My **ten** Book

by Jane Belk Moncure
illustrated by Linda Hohag
and Dan Spoden

THE CHILD'S WORLD

Library of Congress Cataloging in Publication Data

Moncure, Jane Belk.
  My ten book.

(My number books)

  Summary: Little ten plays with her ten robot dolls
and manipulates other toys and items for the reader
to see what numbers can be put together to make ten.
  1. Ten (The number)—Juvenile literature.
[1. Ten (The number) 2. Number concept.   3. Counting]
I. Title.   II. Series: Moncure, Jane Belk.   My number
books.
QA141.3.M675 1986   513'.2 [E]   86-2293
ISBN 0-89565-321-4 -1995 Edition

My  **ten** Book

This is Little **ten**.

Little  **ten** lives in the house of ten.

It has ten rooms. Count them.

Every day Little  goes for a walk.

One day she walks to her mailbox.
She finds a letter.

It says,

January 10
Dear Friend,
I have sent
you ten surprises
for your birthday!
Love,
A secret pal

Soon a truck comes down the road. Guess what is inside?

Little  gets a big box. It says, "Happy Birthday, Little Ten."

Inside the box are ten robot dolls.

"What a super birthday gift," says Little ten.

Little  ten takes the dolls for a ride . . .

in her wagon,

but three dolls fall out! How many
stay in the wagon? Count them.

Little  **ten** takes her dolls for a ride . . .

on her sled,

but five dolls fall off the sled.

How many stay on?

Little  takes her robot dolls home and puts them in . . .

one big playpen.  Do any fall out?

Little ten has fun with her dolls all year long — especially on holidays.

For Valentine's Day, Little  ten makes valentines for them.

First she makes six valentines.

How many more does she need?

On Saint Patrick's Day, she makes green shamrocks for her dolls' hats.

She paints five.
How many more does she need?

My! How nice the dolls look in the
Saint Patrick's Day parade.

Count them two by two.

At Easter time, Little  makes an Easter basket for each doll.

So far she has eight made.

How many more does she need?

Then she hides Easter eggs for her dolls.
How many has she hidden?

On the Fourth of July, Little  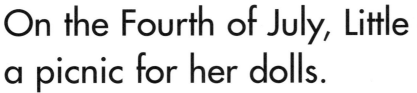 packs a picnic for her dolls.

She makes five big sandwiches.

When she cuts them in half, how many half sandwiches does she have for her dolls?

Count them.

Then she cuts five big apples in half.
Does she have ten pieces? Count them.

On Halloween night, Little  ten has a funny mask for each doll to wear.

She puts masks on two dolls. How many more dolls need masks?

The ten masked dolls go to a friend's house singing, "Trick-or-treat." Seven dolls go inside. How many stay outside?

At Thanksgiving time, Little  makes an Indian wigwam for the dolls.

They play Indians and Pilgrims.
How many play outside the
wigwam?

At Christmas time, Little  hangs a stocking for each doll.

How many more does she need to hang?

How many dolls
help decorate
the tree?

Where are the other seven?

They are wrapping a gift.
Guess whose gift?

On Christmas morning who gives her
ten dolls one great big hug?

Let's add with Little ten .

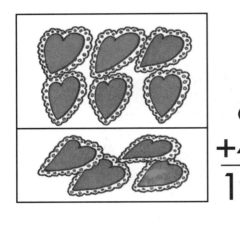

$$\begin{array}{r} 6 \\ +4 \\ \hline 10 \end{array}$$

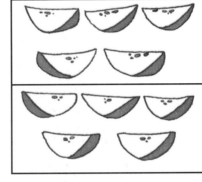

$$\begin{array}{r} 5 \\ +5 \\ \hline 10 \end{array}$$

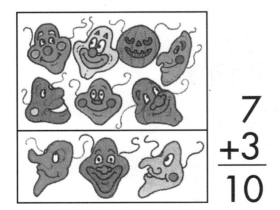

$$\begin{array}{r} 7 \\ +3 \\ \hline 10 \end{array}$$

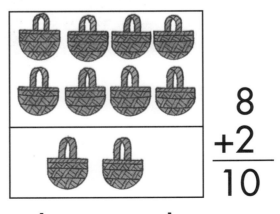

$$\begin{array}{r} 8 \\ +2 \\ \hline 10 \end{array}$$

Now you add ten things together in other ways.

Let's take away with Little  .

$$10$$
$$-3$$
$$\overline{7}$$

$$10$$
$$-1$$
$$\overline{9}$$

$$10$$
$$-8$$
$$\overline{2}$$

$$10$$
$$-5$$
$$\overline{5}$$

Now you take away from ten in other ways.

Extra
Pages

"See what I can do," says Little  .
She makes a 10 this way:

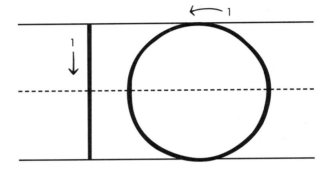

Then she makes the number word like this:

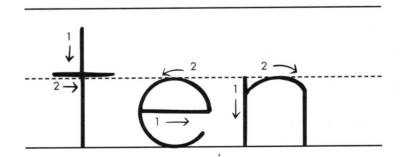

You can make them in the air with your finger.